T0354283

communism
for KIDS

communism for KIDS

bini adamczak

translated by jacob blumenfeld and sophie lewis

the mit press | cambridge, massachusetts | london, england

This translation © 2017 Massachusetts Institute of Technology

This book was set in Helvetica Rounded and Chaparral by The MIT Press. Printed and bound in the United States of America.

Library of Congress Cataloging-in-Publication Data

Names: Adamczak, Bini, author.
Title: Communism for kids / Bini Adamczak ; translated by
    Jacob Blumenfeld and Sophie Lewis.
Other titles: Kommunismus.
English Description: Cambridge, MA : MIT Press, 2017. |
    Includes bibliographical references.
Identifiers: LCCN 2016032230 | ISBN 9780262533355
    (pbk. : alk. paper)
Subjects: LCSH: Communism.
Classification: LCC HX73 .A3313 2017 | DDC 335.43—dc23
    LC record available at https://lccn.loc.gov/2016032230

10   9   8   7   6   5   4   3   2

contents

what is communism?

Communism names the society that gets rid of all the evils people suffer today in our society under capitalism. There are lots of different ideas about what communism should look like. But if communism means getting rid of all the evils people suffer under capitalism, then the best kind of communism is the one that can get rid of the most evils. It's like curing a disease. If capitalism was a disease—which it's *not*—then the best medicine would be the kind of communism that can make people completely well, and not merely one-third or half well. Still, people usually are healthy before they get sick, and medicine just returns them to the way they were at first. That's not really true with capitalism, because people suffered a lot before it, too, although for different reasons. That's why the comparison isn't so good. And even if communism is a good remedy, it's no cure-all. It's only a remedy for the evils caused by capitalism. If you have a cough and fever, and you take a pill for the cough, then only the cough goes away, not the fever. Communism is kind of like that:

it doesn't heal all suffering but rather only the suffering caused by capitalism.

To really understand communism and figure out which idea of it is the best, we have to first understand capitalism and how it makes people suffer.

what is capitalism?

Capitalism exists today all over the world, and it's called capitalism because capital rules. This isn't the same as saying that capitalists rule, or that the capitalist class rules. In capitalism, there are certainly people who have more power than others, but there isn't a queen who sits on a throne high above society and commands everybody. So if people no longer rule over society, who does? The answer may sound a little strange. *Things* do. Of course we don't mean this literally, since things can't do anything, least of all rule people. After all, they're just things. And not all things have this power; only special things do. Or to put it better, only a special form of things do. These special things don't fall from the sky or come flying down to Earth in UFOs shooting people with laser beams. They're just the things that people create to make life easier, to serve them. Strangely, over time, people forget that *they* made those things, and soon enough, people begin to serve the things!

Imagine this: a girl walks over to a desk and writes down on a piece of paper, "Please drink a glass of water." One or two hours later, she wanders by the desk again and finds that piece of paper. As she reads it this time, she forgets that *she* was the one who wrote it and thinks to herself that she should probably do what the paper says. Maybe she's a bit skeptical at first, so she finds a friend and asks, "Do I really *have* to drink a glass of water right now? I'm not even thirsty." The friend answers, "I don't know. Here, let me have a look." She reads what's written on the piece of paper and tells the girl, "Yep, that's what it says. You have to drink a glass of water." If the girl walks by this piece of paper too often, she would get a terrible bellyache pretty quickly. And that's how she ends up being ruled by things and suffering.

Sure enough, this sounds a bit odd. Why should she suddenly forget that she wrote that sentence? Why would she no longer recognize her own handwriting? In general, reality is a bit more complicated than it appears in this scene. People don't live and work alone but rather in society together. In reality, it's never just one person writing down a sentence; it's lots of people writing things together. Let's try a different example—the Ouija board (there's a glass in this one, too). To play the game, a group of people sits in a circle around a board with a glass in the middle. All the letters of the alphabet are written on the board. Everyone puts a hand or finger on the glass, and because everybody is unconsciously trembling a tiny bit, the glass begins to move, as if pushed by an invisible hand, slowly, from one letter to the next. The people don't realize that *they* moved the glass themselves, because their individual trembling could never have moved it alone. Instead, they think it was a spirit channeling some kind of message through them.

The Ouija board illustrates pretty well how life works under capitalism. As a matter of fact, the people playing the game are pushing the magically moving glass all by themselves, although not one of them could do it alone. The glass moves only because people act together rather than separately. But they don't even notice they are cooperating. Their own cooperation happens secretly, behind their backs, so to speak. If those people instead consciously came together to think collectively about what they actually wanted to write, then the outcome would probably be very different. At least, there wouldn't be any uncertainty about who wrote the text, that's for sure. With the way things stand now, though, the text seems to be written by an invisible hand. And since no one can explain how it happened, they believe it was an alien power, like a spirit—or specter.

So you see, it's not every kind of cooperation, every kind of group, or every kind of labor that gives things special powers over people. It's only a special kind. The Ouija board fits, but writing collectively does not. Similarly, things don't rule over every society; that only happens in a capitalist society. Only in capitalism do people relate to each other and work together in a way that leads to things ruling people. But what's so special about the relationships between people under capitalism? What distinguishes them from the relationships people have with each other in different societies?

To answer these questions, let's take a look at how capitalism first came about. When we do, we'll see that capitalism has not always existed (which is already a big plus).

how did capitalism arise?

Capitalism first developed in England around five hundred years ago. At that time, feudalism still ruled, which means there were queens, princesses, and many maids. But most people were peasants. Peasants worked the fields in small village communes or together with their families. Since they had no machines and few inventions, they had to work a ton. Even though they worked so much, they were still poor. Even worse, the church, which was very powerful at that time, demanded every tenth piece of bread the peasants produced—and the princesses wanted even more than that! Every so often, the people had to go to the princesses' courts and work there for several days. But they always knew exactly how much the rulers were taking away from them. Otherwise, they were pretty much left alone. You see, the princesses understood little about working, and so they couldn't really tell the peasants how to do their work.

At the time, England was a great sea power with bustling trade missions all across the world. Many merchant ships left every morning from

the English docks to Africa, Europe, and far-away lands like Asia and America. Since there weren't many merchants with big enough ships and heavy enough artillery to do all this, the ones who had the ships did good business. They sailed, for example, to America, where they stole all the jewelry from the people living there and then sold it in Europe. Then they sailed to Africa, stole the people living there, and sold them in America. These merchants became rich and soon enjoyed a kind of luxury the princesses could never imagine even in their wildest dreams.

When the princesses saw how rich the merchants had become with their gigantic jewels and fancy swords, they grew jealous. They feared that the merchants, having become so economically powerful, would demand lots more political influence or even overthrow the princesses—which later, in fact, they did.

The princesses feverishly plotted how they, too, could become rich like the merchants. But the only thing they really owned was the land that the peasants lived on, and the turnips the peasants grew on the land never earned them much money. More money could be made with sheep's wool, which was valuable at the time in Europe. And so the princesses called out to all their underlings and ordered them to stop growing turnips, and instead to breed sheep everywhere.

Now as it turns out, it takes far less peasants to care for sheep than it does to grow turnips. And when sheep are everywhere, a lot less people can survive on the land. That's how the vast majority of peasants became unnecessary.

The princesses cared little about what happened to the peasants, since they only had eyes for the merchants' fancy swords and gigantic jewels. And so the princesses sent their soldiers to kick the peasants off the land where they had always lived and always worked. The soldiers were rude and hurt the peasants a lot. At first the peasants were pretty upset. Yet imagine how much sadder they became when they realized that they could never return back to their land—and that everything they had ever learned was now useless. None of them had any clue how to support themselves anymore. Since they didn't know where else to go, they moved to the big cities. But when they arrived, they saw huge crowds of former peasants already living there—peasants who'd also been driven off their land. Without land, none of them could grow any food. And since they didn't own anything, they had nothing to sell either. Of course, they could always steal, but then the police might catch and punish them. The only thing they still had was themselves. And so the people went to the factories and sold themselves.

Since then, all people in capitalism—at least, those who don't happen to own a factory—have been forced to sell themselves. Otherwise they have no money and can't buy anything to eat. Everybody wants to eat, and so we have to go to work whether we like it or not. We have to make things—guns, for example—whether we think they're stupid or not. And just like that, things rule people. Funnily, not many soldiers and police officers are needed to keep this all going.

As it turns out, work is a big deal in capitalism. Everything depends on it. People who don't work can't eat. And people who don't work aren't really liked by others—because some people believe that they just mooch off all the things that other people make. To better understand how capitalism works, we have to take a closer look at this so-called work.

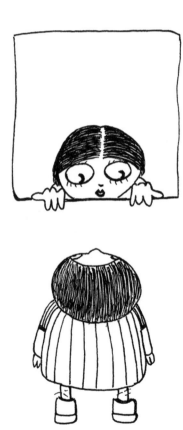

what is work?

Every morning, before it's even time to go to school, people get up to go to the factory or office. Many only go in the afternoon, and many more only begin at night; some are even allowed, nowadays, to decide for themselves when they go to work. Others work at home, clearing the breakfast table and ironing clothes. But this doesn't matter, since in any case, they all have to work. As soon as people reach the gate of a factory or doorway to an office, a clerk greets them and asks, "Do you want to work for our factory or our office?" And what can the people say? Most likely, they're not interested in working, and would much rather have stayed in bed a bit longer or meet up with friends for breakfast. But they better keep that to themselves, because they know that they can only afford breakfast if they have a job.

So they say, "Yes, I do."

"Very good," says the clerk in her polite tone of voice. "The factory," she continues, "will give you enough money to eat and drink and pay your rent, and also go to the movies twice a week. But

in exchange, you have to do pretty much everything the factory tells you to do for as long as
you're here."

"Movies twice a week sounds great," the people tell themselves, "but doing everything the
factory tells me to do, for as long as I'm here,
eight hours a day? That's a third of my day! And
if I sleep for eight hours, that's half the time I'm
awake! That really adds up, all just to go to the
movies twice a week."

But what else can they say? They've already
agreed in principle, and besides, they're already
standing at the door of the factory or office.

They have barely shut the door behind them
when the factory begins shouting.

"Come along this hallway!" the factory beck-
ons in its booming voice. "And now, go straight
through that door. Do you see the chair over
there? Sit yourself down on it." The factory
pauses and thinks for a moment before carry-
ing on: "Well, well, well, what have we got here?
Today, precisely 1,223 steam irons have to be
made. That is why, every hour, you have to bang
this nail a hundred times."

"Huh? I have to bang this stupid nail? A hundred times?" one worker angrily protests. "But
why? What on earth is that good for? What
does it have to do with the steam irons? And

who wants so many irons anyway? Who needs so many irons?"

But the factory voice is already gone. It has much more important things to do than answer the questions of its workers. What's more, it probably doesn't even know the answers.

Of course the factory doesn't really speak with an actual voice. It's only a factory—made up of stones, machines, and plastic. It has no mouth at all. Despite this, the factory does speak with its own special voice. We can understand this better with another example. Think of a chair. If you never saw a chair before, and if you had no idea what a chair was, then you wouldn't really know what to do with it once you saw one. Maybe you would try to light a fire with it. Or maybe you would try to sleep under it. But as soon as you know what a chair is, maybe because somebody explained it to you, then you would also understand the chair's own language. The chair says stuff like "Sit yourself down here, like this. No, you can't lie on me; you'll fall over! And stop your wobbling, or else you'll break my hind legs." If the chair is an uncomfortable one, then it will probably say mean things like "Aww, does this hurt? I'm gonna prick you now and give you back pain!" At work and in schools, the chairs are mostly nasty chairs of that type. They

make themselves stiff on purpose, so that you can only sit on them in one position. They don't want people to feel too comfortable and doze off to sleep for even an instant.

Where were we? Oh yes, the factory. Over time, people have built lots and lots of large factories. Unfortunately, they never shut up. Now we have to listen to them all the time. The factories are always talking about the same three things. They tell us *how* we should produce, *what* we should produce, and *how much* we should produce. For instance, the factory tells some workers to sit around a table in a group and discuss something all night long; it tells another group to pass different things back and forth to each other until the morning. The factory tells some workers to stay at home all day and do the ironing. It tells other workers to hammer nails, and another group to turn a computer on and off, and then write nonstop about a bunch of stuff the factory dreams up. There are even workers who have to design pistols. The factory also announces how much it wants of everything. For example, a hundred nails hammered per hour, or one entire apartment's laundry pressed, or five pages written daily on the computer. Finally, the factory decides how much everyone should get in return for doing all this work. Maybe one movie ticket for hammering nails, no movie tickets for washing laundry, and a hundred tickets for playing the boss.

Now one worker might not want to hammer all day long but would much rather write—preferably only four pages a day, not five. And another worker might not want to just do the ironing but would much rather sit around a table with other people, or better yet, do a little bit of everything throughout the day. Iron at home in the morning, sit around a table in the afternoon, and write beautiful poems in the evening. And a third worker isn't really sure what she'd like to do exactly but she doesn't want anything to do with pistols—that's for certain.

But when the workers show up at the factory and make these suggestions, the factory suddenly plays deaf, acting like it doesn't understand anything. It's only a factory, silly, made up of stones, machines, and plastic. Factories don't have ears. Sighing, the people turn around and return to their jobs. They realize that although people built the factory, it doesn't really care about people. It doesn't care if they're happy, or if they know what they're making and why. The only thing the factory cares about is making and selling as much stuff as possible. The factory only wants people to be happy if being happy sells more stuff. And if being happy really does sell more stuff, then the people *have* to be happy—even if they're really not. And that makes them unhappy. More stuff is sold, though, and that's the only thing the factory cares about. If the factory can sell lots of stuff, then it can buy some more workers and extra machines, and then it can produce even more steam irons, texts, or pistols. And then the factory can sell those, too.

If the factory doesn't care about people, and if the people are only supposed to care about what the factory cares about, and if the factory only cares about buying and selling, then buying and selling must be pretty darn important.

To better understand how the factory works, we have to take a closer look at what the factory is doing when it sells things in order to buy things only in order to sell things again. To sell and buy things, the factory has to go to the marketplace. This is not a tiny village marketplace with fruit and vegetable stands. For factories, there are special, huge marketplaces. Let's take a closer look.

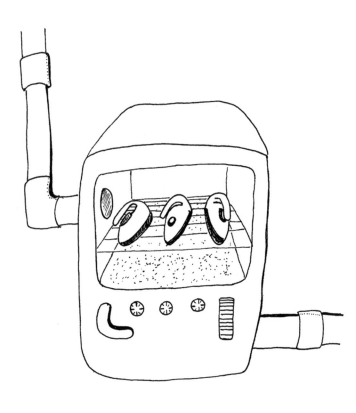

what is the market?

Before the factory can sell anything on the market, it first has to make something. Making or producing something requires various ingredients—like baking a cake. To bake a cake, we need: 1. eggs, sugar, and flour; 2. an oven; and 3. a baker. But our factory doesn't want to bake cakes; it wants to make steam irons. So it buys a large heap of sheet metal and a big sack of nails. Making an iron out of sheet metal and nails requires a huge iron-making machine. So the factory buys three gigantic steam-iron-making machines. Altogether that's three huge iron-making machines, a big sack of nails, and a fat stack of sheet metal in the factory. Yet for some reason, nothing moves. All of a sudden it occurs to the factory that it still needs one more thing: those people, the *workers*!

There's a special market where factories go to pick up workers: the labor market. At the labor market, there are lots of different people on sale who have already been produced ready-made in other special factories, like the school and family factories. That's why our factory can go to the labor market and place an exact order for the kind of people it needs. It says, "Good morning, I need twelve nail-hammering-people, six sheet-metal-bending people, and one iron-testing-person." In addition to them, the factory needs two thinking people who can think up the formula for how to make steam irons out of machines, sheet metal, nails, and people. Finally, it needs a boss person who makes sure everybody does what the factory wants them to do. The factory asks the people, "Do you want to work for me?" And the people say, "Yes, we do." But we already heard all about that.

Next the factory takes the people it bought at the labor market, comes home, and locks them inside together with the sheet metal, machines, and nails—every day for eight hours. Lo and behold, after a while the first freshly baked irons begin to pop out of the factory. The factory takes those irons back to the market and sells them. This time it doesn't go to the labor market but instead to the irons market, or the Irons-and-MORE market. When the factory sells its irons there, it receives money. And with that money it can buy itself sheet metal, nails, iron-making people, and all the newest machines. And with the new machines, sheet metal, nails, and iron-making people, it can make even more new irons. And it can sell those all over again.

While at the Irons-and-MORE market, the factory daydreams about what factories always daydream about: new machines, sheet metal, nails, and iron-making people. One day, all of a sudden, it stops and notices something. Not so far away, just across the street to be exact, there's another factory *also selling irons*. "I need to take a closer look at this," mutters our factory, and takes a closer look. It spots the prices for these other irons and thinks to itself, "This can't be happening." For what should it see? The other factory is selling irons at a cheaper price! Not a great deal cheaper, but just enough to make a difference, since people are already buying more irons from *them*.

"Damn, damn, damn!" our factory thinks (factories are terribly jealous, if you didn't know already). It simply can't stand the fact that the other factory is selling cheaper irons. And more of them, too! In fact, it can't stand the other factory, period. Come to think of it, factories can't stand anyone or anything, especially workers or other factories.

The only thing that makes factories happy is selling and buying, and selling and buying. And the only thing they dream about is machines, sheet metal, nails, and iron-making people. You would think that our factory could easily walk up to the other factory and say, "Hey friend, how do you make those irons so darn cheap? I want to do that, too." Or maybe: "Well, isn't this a coincidence? You and I both make steam irons! How about we do it together? That would make a lot more sense, wouldn't it?" But factories don't think like that, and if they do team up, it's only to annoy a third factory.

Where were we? Oh right, our factory is *furious*. Once it has returned home, it immediately calls its two thinking people over and asks them what to do.

"You'll have to make steam irons cheaper and faster, and more of them, too. You'll have to cut costs so that you can sell them at a lower price. For instance," says the first thinking person, "you really only need one thinking-person, not two."

"That's a great idea," says the factory—and fires the first thinking person on the spot.

The next day, the factory gathers together all its iron-making people (minus one thinking person) and announces,

"From now on, you'll only get enough money to go to the movies once a week. Also, you'll have to work one extra hour per day."

The people don't like this one bit, but they've already learned that the factory always plays deaf when they try to speak to it. And so drooping their heads, they go back to work.

A few weeks later, our factory returns to the market with a swagger, showing off its brand-new super-cheap irons. "Gather round, people!" it shouts. "My irons are much cheaper than those ones over *there*." And with its large metal fingers, it points to the other factory across the street, gloating the whole time. It's a pretty clever move. Everybody crowds around our factory, buying up the irons. Meanwhile, the other factory sells less and less. Our factory is delighted. While selling the irons, it sometimes shuts its big window-eyes and dreams of all the new machines, stacks of sheet metal, heaps of nails, and iron-making people it will buy with all its new money.

But what's that sorry sight across the street? That's the other factory, perched crookedly on top of all the irons it can no longer sell. If we look a little closer, we can see thick black tears of soot dripping slowly from its chimney. This factory, it turns out, had lots of debt and hadn't been doing so well after all. Now that our factory makes cheaper steam irons, this other factory can't sell any of its steam irons anymore. And since it can't sell irons any longer, it can't buy new machines, sheet metal, nails, or iron-making people either. The other factory is very, very sad—and then goes bankrupt. It all happens so fast! Because it's broke, the bankrupt factory fires all its workers. All the other iron-making people are now suddenly unemployed. And even though they thought working there was pretty stupid, they're still unhappy, because now they won't get any money and won't be able to go to the movies.

Before, the workers from both factories were able to go to the movies twice a week. Now, one group of workers can only go to the movies once a week while the other group can't go at all. But there's something else. People who can't afford to go to the movies also can't afford to shop for irons. And that leads to a big problem.

To understand why there are more and more things lying around that nobody can afford (like irons), we need to take a closer look at this problem called *crisis*.

what is crisis?

The next time our factory goes to the market, it brings twice as many steam irons as it did before, thinking to itself, "The other factory is bankrupt. Fantastic! Now everyone who used to buy irons there will come to me instead. I'll have twice as many customers, so I'll need twice as many irons." Imagine the surprise when it sees nobody waiting at the Irons-and-MORE marketplace. Almost nobody wants to buy irons anymore—anywhere. What happened on the street between our factory and the other factory also happened everywhere in the world. There are countless factories out there: not just those that make irons, but also those that produce pistols, create candy, build baseballs, and more. Now that people only go to the movies once a week or not at all, they don't feel like buying irons. Instead, they stay at home and watch movies on television, or play games on their phone. It's not the same, they tell themselves, but it's better than nothing.

Other people have it even worse. Not only can't they go to the movies anymore, they don't even have enough to eat! Some of them decide to buy tomatoes and eggs, and throw them at the factory walls, because that seems like a good idea. The factory, though, has no use for tomatoes, since it's an iron factory, not a factory for making tomato sauce. It's stuck with all these darn irons. Stupidly, the factory brought twice as many irons as usual to the market today. But it can't sell twice as many irons; it can only get itself into twice as much debt. Sure enough, our factory goes bankrupt just like the other one did. And it fires all the iron-making people.

Now there's nothing left. No factories, no machines, no sheet metal or nails, and no iron-making people. But there are still vast piles of irons that nobody needs. Although no terrible disaster has occurred—no earthquake, no war, and no visit from the pope—all of a sudden, everyone is just sitting around, bored stiff and hungry as hell. Some are trying to turn their irons into a stew, but that's proving pretty pointless. "We're in a real mess now," the people say. "If only we hadn't listened to these factories!" And one person adds, "You know what? It's all these *things*! We make them in order to serve us, but then, they start getting all smug and saucy, and we end up serving them. Now we're stuck hanging around all these damn steam irons." And another one adds, really angrily now, "I knew it! It's these dumb thingamajigs, this damned thinga- ... thinga- ... thingification. Blech!"

Everybody sits down around the irons to think long and hard about capitalism, because they've realized that the mess is really all capitalism's fault. "Well, that didn't work out so well," they think to themselves. "First, capitalism made us all unhappy, and then it just kept on going wrong." "And another thing," someone comments loudly, "we've had capitalism long enough now—about five hundred years—so isn't it time for a change? I want something new." "Yes, something new! But what?" asks somebody else. At this point there is a long silence as the people turn over the question in their heads. Each one of them would love to know the answer.

Suddenly it comes to them. "Communism!" they exclaim. "Obviously! Since communism names the society that gets rid of all the evils we suffer under capitalism. Let's try communism!" "Oh," the people groan, "of course." And they all slap their foreheads, because it's so obvious once somebody has finally said it. "Why didn't we think of that before?"

The people now know two things. First, they know that capitalism doesn't make them happy, and second, they know that communism does. So they decide to try communism. But it's not so simple. Since true communism has never existed in the entire history of humankind, no one has any clue what it looks like. What the people do have are various ideas of what a communist society *should* look like. If communism names the society that gets rid of all the evils people suffer under capitalism, then the best kind of communism is the one that gets rid of the most evils. In order to figure out the best kind of communism, the people have to see which of these ideas could get rid of *all* the evils people suffer under capitalism—not just one-third or half of them. No one really knows unless they try it out. "We'd better try out these ideas one by one," the people decide. "Then we'll see."

And so they begin.

what is to be done?

trial no. 1

"First of all," the people say, "we'd better think about what actually went wrong. If we can figure that out, then we can do it better. It's not like everything has to change all at once." Sitting around the heap of irons, they realize that although society is rich, nobody has anything to show for it. What a shame! There are so many irons lying around, and nobody can buy them. Nobody has enough money even to go to the movies anymore. "That's it!" they say. "If we had more money, then we could have *bought* the irons. And if we had bought the irons, then the factories would have had enough money to make new ones. And the factories would have needed new machines, new sheet metal and nails, and new iron-making people, ... and then we wouldn't have lost our jobs."

The reason they had so little money was because the factories had taken it away from them. How, then, should they get their hands on more money? "Since the factories took the money from the people, we should take it back from the factories," somebody suggests. "That's a good idea," says another. "But how should we do it?" "The best way," a third person replies, "is for us to find a huge pot. Each of us will put a little of our money into this pot. Those who have a lot of money will put a lot in, and those who have a little will put a little in. Then we'll share the money from the pot with the people, but the other way around: those who have a little get a lot, and those who have a lot get a little." "Better yet," says somebody else, "let's make it even easier and buy the extra irons with the money right from the pot. That's even simpler."

And so they do it. Everybody has to pay into the big pot, except that they call the pot the "state," because it sounds better that way. Everyone can now go to the movies twice a week again, at least in theory. In reality, lots of people still can only go to the movies once a week or not at all. Yet that doesn't matter, since the pot— or rather, the state—simply buys the leftover movie tickets every night. The same goes for the irons. There are still people who have none, but no worries: the pot has the rest. And since the pot—that is, the state—buys everything that the people can't afford, the factories always have plenty of money, and can give out lots of work to movie-ticket makers and iron-making people.

Everybody's happy, since they can all come back every day to the factory and ... work. But *"just a minute!"* someone interrupts. "Working in the factory isn't fun at all! It's exactly the same dumb work as before." It's true. The people still work exactly as much as the factory demands. And so when all's said and done, not much has changed. "That's not how we imagined it," the people say, shaking their heads. "No, no, no. This isn't communism."

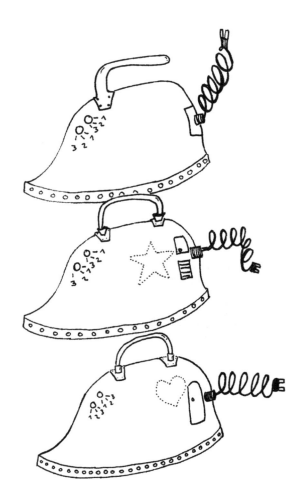

trial no. 2

The people sit back down and think it all over again. The irons are all gone now, but the machines and factories are still there, along with the sheet metal and nails. Everyone's sitting and thinking, thinking and sitting, until finally someone says, "The important thing isn't *that* irons are made but rather *how* they are made. It's not enough just to have some work to do. What matters is the *kind* of work we are doing." "Yes! That's right," calls out someone else. "Who cares if I have work when I don't enjoy it? Why do I have to run around in a circle all day long, alone? And why does my neighbor have to sit around a table all night? And why does this woman over here have to think all the time and play the boss?" "It can't go on like this," the people agree. "We cannot have the factory telling us when, how, and how long we're supposed to work. From now on, we decide for ourselves."

And so they do it. The people return to their factories. Only now they don't make what the factories tell them to make; they make whatever they want to make. To show everyone that the factory belongs to those who work it, they hang little black-and-red flags out of the factory's windows. Every morning, the people sit down together in a big circle and discuss how they want to work that day. Each person can choose what they want to do, and everyone is allowed to do everything, except there are no boss persons anymore. It will take some considerable time for everybody to *really* be able to do everything: bend metal, hammer nails, and think deeply. Because of course it's easier in some ways to just do one thing forever.

Yet little by little, the people learn. And it's not too long before the first irons come out of the factory. All the irons are now made with a great deal of love and care. Each one looks a little bit different than the rest. You can even find tiny red hearts and little black stars painted on some of them.

In the morning, the two iron-making people who were chosen to be iron salespeople for the day get up and go to the market with the irons. When they get there they see, once again, two iron salespeople from the other iron factory across the street. And they are, once again, selling irons at a cheaper price! "This can't be true," our iron salespeople cry. "It's so unfair." They walk over to the other iron salespeople to talk to them and tell them that they should be selling their irons at a higher price. But the other iron salespeople won't be reasonable! "We are all free people now," comes their retort. "It's our factory, and we alone decide how cheaply we will sell our irons here. Also, we have a longer way to travel to the market than you do, so we have some extra costs to make up."

Our iron salespeople go home again, feeling sad. They gather all the other iron-making people together and tell them what happened at the market. Naturally, everybody becomes sad. "Oh dear! If we want to keep our factory running, we'll have to produce more cheaply, too, or else no one will buy from us." Up until then, the iron-making people had been putting all the money they earned into a little potty, and everyone received the same amount out of it. But since they now want to sell their irons at a cheaper price, they can't spend as much money as they are used to. To save money, they decide to lay off two of their fellow iron-making people. "And while we're at it," they mumble, "it might be better, after all, if we pick someone to be a boss person—someone who can tell us what to do next. It doesn't always have to be the same person." So the iron-making people make one of their own into a boss person. And then they use a lottery to choose which two people to lay off. Fair's fair.

The next day, the two poor ex-iron-making persons, now unemployed, pack their things and leave the factory. The others gather to say farewell and wave them off with their handkerchiefs. There's not a dry eye among them, but nonetheless, those two have to go. There's just nothing to do about it. They'll probably make their way over to the pistol-making plant—supposedly, there are still some jobs there.

Still huddled together, the people of the factory pause and take stock: "Inside our factory, we're free. We can decide collectively on what we want to do each day. But at the marketplace, we're still forced to compete against each other. At the marketplace, we have to sell our irons *even if* it makes other people suffer. It's true, we can now decide on how we want to work. But we have no control over what we make or how much. That's not how we imagined it," the people say, shaking their heads. "No, no, no. This isn't communism."

trial no. 3

Once more, the people are sitting around all together, trying to come up with a good idea. At this point, the crowd has swollen to a mass. It's not just the people from our iron-making factory but the people from other iron-making factories as well. And it's not just them either but also people from the movie-ticket-printing factory, the pistol-making plant, and more! There are so many people now that you really have to shout if you want anyone to hear you. But that's not all. Somehow, the people feel different. Somehow, the people have changed. Without bosses, they've had to do everything all by themselves. They've become much, much smarter. Since they've been deciding in common every morning what they want to do, they've learned how to listen to each other. If someone doesn't like something, they simply say so. No one thinks for others anymore; everyone thinks for themselves. And so it's not long before the first ideas on how to finally make communism start to bubble. "In

our factory, things were going fairly well," someone remarks. "We talked to each other a lot and
decided everything together in common. We
stopped doing what the factories wanted, and
the factories started doing what we wanted.

"But at the marketplace," another person chips
in, "things were totally different. At the marketplace, people only opened their mouths to say
stuff like 'One iron, please!' or 'How much for
this iron?' or 'Do you have such and such an iron?'
We always answered them with phrases like 'Of
course' or 'The iron costs so much' or 'No, unfortunately, we don't have such and such an iron.'
Everything revolved around *things*." Things! This
really riles the people up because they don't want
to be ruled anymore, especially not by things.

They continue: "We never actually knew how
many irons or movie tickets to make, because
we never actually knew how many things the
people really needed." "Right," others say, "some
factories had good luck and happened to make
exactly what the people wanted. Others had
much worse luck, and nobody wanted to buy
their stuff. That's why some people became
rich, and others poor." This is obviously unfair.
It makes everyone so mad because they had
set aside special little potties of money in each
of their factories just so that everybody would
get the same amount. Yet thinking of pots, an

idea pops into their heads. The people have that big old pot, the state, which nobody was using lately. "We still have the *big* pot!" they cry. "Why don't we pool all our money into the big pot and agree that everyone gets the same amount out?" "Now that's a good idea!" shout the others. "That would actually be fair." "But we also have to arrange everything a bit better. If we only check at the marketplace to see whether the things we made are really needed by others, then it's already too late. It would make more sense if the people who collect and distribute the pot money can also figure out what stuff we need. Then they could tell the people in the factory exactly how much to make."

And so they do it. When people come into the factory at noon the next day, they find a hefty wish list lying there ready for them. The pot people placed it there. Everyone can add to the wish list by writing down the things they need. The pot people then pass by to pick up the wish list and carefully add the items up. Then they tell all the factories what the people need and how much should be produced. And at the end of the month, everyone receives equal amounts of money from the pot. The people prefer to call the pot a "pot" instead of a state, because it's really supposed to be nothing more than just a pot. With help from the pot, everyone can buy the same amount of stuff. From now on, there are no longer people who can go to the movies eight days a week, and others who can only go once a week. Now everyone can go to the movies five days a week. Everyone loves this idea because everyone loves going to the movies. During the day, the people make the things they eat in the evening. And the pot people take care of the administration of things.

The people live like this for a good while. But eventually, the pot people become weary of dealing with the wish lists. The factory people want far more than what the pot people can provide to them. That's because not enough things are being made. So the pot people tell the factory people that they have to work harder and longer in order to make enough stuff to fulfill all the wish lists. Meanwhile, the wish lists grow longer and longer. The people have so many wishes, and so everyone has to work more and more. And it's not only more work but also harder and faster work. The people in the factories start to grunt and groan, because they no longer have any time during work to play a game of dice or take a nap. The pot people demand that they work harder, though. Before you know it, work has become as exhausting and boring as it was before, under capitalism.

At this point, the people could meet up and say, "We don't want to work so hard. Why don't we just wish for a little less, so that we don't end up exhausting ourselves like this?" But the only places where the people meet are the factories and movie theaters. And when they're there, they would much rather talk about other things. It ends up that people really only tell their wishes to the wish lists. They no longer decide together what they need; they no longer think together about how much to make. Each person decides alone. And that's why nobody thinks about wishing for less. They assume that everybody else is wishing for lots of things anyway, so no matter what, they'll have to work more.

Only the pot people know for sure how much is being wished for and how much has to be made. And since pot people are also people with wishes of their own, they begin to place their personal wish lists at the top of the pile. At first, they only do this once in a while, in secret. Yet slowly, they start do it a little bit more, and then a little bit more, and then all the time. At the end of most days, the wishes of the pot people are the most satisfied. Since they're the only ones who know the wishes and needs of everybody, the pot people can easily influence what's made and how much. And so they grow richer and more powerful, while the factory people work longer and harder only to see their wishes fulfilled less and less. And the people say, "We wanted to figure out everything for ourselves, together. But now it's only pot people figuring everything out. Instead of talking with each other, we only speak to our wish lists." "Exactly," interject some other people angrily, rubbing their backs, which ache from all the hard work they've been doing. "We're no longer ruled by things, but now we're ruled by people all over again. This isn't much better. That's not how we imagined it," the people say, shaking their heads. "No, no, no. This isn't communism."

trial no. 4

The people are sitting together again, this time in a movie theater. But no movies are showing today, because they really need to talk about what happened. It seems that making communism is not so easy after all. "It's not so easy after all," the people think. "If we want to stop being ruled by things, we better not end up being ruled by people again." "Yeah," says another, "communist society should get rid of all the evils people suffer under capitalism. But if we're not careful, we could bring back the evils of past societies. The pot people just now were acting like the princesses of old." And so they think really hard about how not to be ruled by people again, whether pot people, boss people, or princesses. "Making so many things and fulfilling so many wishes was pretty nice," the people say, "but work was killing us." "Well then," somebody suggests, "let's get rid of work." "Excellent idea!" other people exclaim. "Why didn't we think of this before? Let the machines do the work for us!"

And so they do it. Now the machines are working instead of people. Since the people are no longer afraid of being unemployed, it's not a problem when the machines take their jobs. In fact, they look forward to it, because now they have more free time to enjoy. The people shout, "Our whole lives, we've been workers. From now on, we're pleasure seekers!" Everyone feels rich. The machines are making more and more things, and not just any old things but instead fancy things that used to be made only for rich people. More than that, the machines are making things that nobody could have imagined under capitalism. Everyone becomes an expert in pleasure seeking. But at the same time, they grow a little lazy. No one really meets up with each other, and no one really talks that much anymore. After all, what should they talk about? The machines are taking care of everything. Everyone would rather lie around all day long, bored out of their minds. When they open their mouths, grape juice pours directly onto their tongues, and roasted pigeons made of tofu fall from the sky. Yet the people aren't so happy.

Lying there, a thought crosses their minds. Once again, everything revolves around things! People only care about having enough things. And nothing remains of the new and extraordinary skills they developed while doing everything for themselves in the factories. "We wanted to do everything by ourselves, to decide for ourselves, and not be ruled by anybody or anything," the people complain. "But now we don't do anything together anymore. And people only speak to their things, not to each other. That's not how we imagined it," the people say, shaking their heads once more. "No, no ... ," they say, but they're interrupted midsentence, because as soon as they open their mouths, roasted pigeons fall in.

trial no. 5

The people are now lying around the fallen snacks, puddles of grape juice, and mounds of extra movie tickets. With great difficulty, they find their feet again. Struggling to stand up, they try to think hard. There's a problem, though; they're almost as dumb now as they were before, under capitalism. That's why their first suggestions aren't so good. "I got it," somebody says. "When everyone receives the same amount of stuff, nobody has any incentive to work. That's why we all got lazy. The solution is simple: everybody should get exactly as many things as they themselves make."

And so they—wait, not so fast! The people are coming to their senses. They remember to speak out when something doesn't feel right. "This is not a good idea," somebody squeals. "Some people can't work as hard as others. And some people don't need as many things as others because their needs are different. Just because some people can work faster and harder than others doesn't mean they should get more stuff. That's unfair."

"That's right!" says another. "Besides, everything would still revolve around these stupid *things*; we're obsessed with how many things each of us makes and each of us gets. Once again, we're ignoring the main question: How do we want to live?" Just like that, the people become so enraged at the things scattered around them that they all grab hammers and smash everything to little pieces. It takes quite some time to do this, because there really are so many things around.

When they're finally done, they're completely exhausted and have to sit down again. This time, however, the people aren't sitting on top of heaps of irons, roasted tofu pigeons, and movie tickets. This time, they're sitting on the wreckage of broken irons, squashed pigeons, and crumpled movie tickets. It's not much better. From afar, it looks as though everyone has become incredibly polite because they're constantly bowing down before each other. But it's just an illusion; if you look closer, you'll see that everyone is bending down to gather weeds and berries growing in the wreckage. The truth is, without things, the people are suddenly poor. The only way to satisfy their hunger is to gather wild berries. So the people stand up once again and rub their aching backs. "That's not how we imagined it," the people say, shaking their heads. "No, no, no. This isn't communism."

trial no. 6

Eventually, the people get sick of all these trials. So they sit down again for a long time to think in peace. But before they begin, they put up long telephone lines and build powerful Internet servers so that all the people in the whole world can take part in making decisions together. After several days of intense conversation, this is what they have to say: "Well, communism names the society that gets rid of all the evils people suffer under capitalism. And that means we have to get rid of *all* the evils of capitalism, not just one-third or half of them. That can't be so hard." "Yep! That's right!" crackles another group of voices on the telephone. "Actually, we got pretty close. But we have to make sure that we don't allow ourselves to be ruled again by other people. And we also don't want to be ruled by things. Not by factories, not by steam irons, not by markets, and not even by movie tickets." "OK, but how do we do it?" asks a different group of people. There are so many people on earth that the conversation almost never ends. "When we smashed all the things to pieces, it became even worse for us."

On that note, another long silence descends, and the people think more intensely than ever. Suddenly it comes to them: "Of course! It's just like the Ouija board. There's no magic without the glass, but there's even less magic without *us*. The glass didn't move because of an invisible hand but rather because we cooperated together." "Yes indeed!" the other people gasp. "That's it. We made everything ourselves—the factories, irons, and movie tickets. All these things are as much a part of us as we are a part of them. That means we can change them whenever we want."

"That's the way!" exclaim the people in triumph. "From now on, there shouldn't be iron-making people or movie-ticket makers anymore. There shouldn't be pistol people or writing people. Instead of factory people, let there be people factories, and instead of machine people, let there be cyborgs! And nobody should work in a single factory anymore. Everyone should be able to do everything and live everywhere."

And so they do it. People can now try everything out. They play and learn together with everyone on the planet because they want to understand everything. If anything seems bad or harmful, they just change it. It's not so easy what they're doing, but it's not so hard either.

Everyone is now having meetings about everything. They're pretty much meeting all the time, since they have to discuss everything themselves. They don't want to leave any decision to some pot person—even though pot people don't exist anymore. The people are now changing everything themselves, as often as they want. "We decide together what we want and then we see who wants to make it," some people explain. "No, it's the other way around," someone else responds. "First we see how long and how fast we want to work, or if we want to work at all. Then we see which needs can be met." As you can see, the people don't always agree. You could even say they're all quite different—more different than before. But they can handle that pretty well. It even makes them happy that there are so many differences between them. Otherwise, it would get boring pretty fast. Finally, the people stop shaking their heads, and instead of saying "no," they start to say—*HELLO*—!

–Hey! Hello! You, over there!
–What? Who me?
I can't believe it. There's some people standing right here at the bottom of the page, peering through the screen right back at me. They're waving their arms in the air and yelling about something. Some of them seem pretty angry.

–Yeah, that's right! You! We mean you. Stop telling our story! We decide what happens next. Because this is our story now, and we're making history ourselves.

epilogue: communist desire

The end of history has ended. When political scientist Francis Fukuyama announced "the end of history" in 1992, he simply meant that there was no alternative to liberal capitalism—forever. It did not take forever for this narrative to be challenged as bourgeois ideology—in 1994 by the Zapatistas in Chiapas, in 1999 by the anti-globalization movement in Seattle, and in 2001 in Genoa. Still, the end-of-history narrative gave expression to a certain undeniable reality. Even the critique of this narrative seemed to confirm its truth. For at no other point in history had the slogan "another world is possible" succeeded in luring people out onto the streets in such force. While the pressing question in other eras was about *which* world among possible worlds would be the most desirable one, and *when* it might finally arrive, the prevalent question was now, Would there be an alternative to the present at all? The end of history depicted a world-historical reality that emerged after the collapse of the Soviet Union and came to be confirmed again ten years later on September 11, 2001. It changed the central motive by which competing political visions legitimized themselves: instead of hope for a better future, there's only a totalizing fear of a worsening present. And this present, which steadily worsened the lives of the majority, stretched out over the horizon seemingly forever.

While living in the present of the "end of history," how can we write about the end of prehistory, about communism? How can we speak of communism in the postcommunist era without surrendering to a powerless pathos? These questions animated this book when it was first published in Germany 2004. For quite some time, history has not been on the side of the communists. The objective sound of triumph has passed. No one regards the laws of history or the laws of nature as our allies anymore. Such views are anachronistic, embarrassing even, along with the moralizing language of agitational manifestos and revolutionary ballads. The objective course of history is an experience of defeat. Nobody is willing to be carried away by grand gestures any longer, and reasonably so. That's the underlying truth about the end of grand narratives. Impulsive gesticulating and raised voices can easily lead to toppling over the edge of the palace railings into the courtyards where no audience is waiting to cushion the fall.

There is no need for soapboxing when there is no public.

After 1990, the atmosphere changed. No longer was anticommunism the main ideology against which a communist text had to situate itself. For the first time in a while, one did not have to take part in class struggle with intellectual weapons. Whether communism would be a better, fairer, more efficient, and more rational form of society was no longer on the agenda, because communism itself was no longer on the agenda. Before attempting to show that communism might be *feasible*, one has to first present it as *conceivable*. Communism needs to be *imaginable* in order to be *desirable*.

If "communism is the *real* movement which abolishes the present state of things," then what could it be under conditions of the absence of such a movement?[1] And what does the movement of communist criticism do when it can't find its adequate communist movement? Shouldn't it above all renounce the asceticism of pure critique? Shouldn't it lend an artificial body to a disembodied theory—one made of silicon and wire? Our historical conjuncture forces us to turn the language of communism back toward the banality of everyday life, toward what's tangible. If communist criticism aspires to move beyond its habit of bitter negation, then it needs to add a blueprint of desire to its toolbox of analytic scalpels and rhetorical dynamite. It needs to generate desire—communist desire.

But doesn't this fall into the trap of utopianism? Isn't the desire for a better life always shaped by the present conditions in which it's constructed? Even if wishes, dreams, ideas, and needs can feed off society's contradictions and develop a progressive "surplus," they can't free themselves completely from the material conditions out of which they grow. They cannot truly be the thoughts, ideas, and images of a different reality, a different organization of society. The question of what communism is and what it will look like is thus prematurely suspected of extending the status quo beyond the boundaries of the present. Utopian fantasies always carry the danger of turning into plans that must be fulfilled, ideals that must be realized. An image of the future becomes a model for the future; description falls prey to prescription.

We shouldn't shy away from this. The current state of the world forces us to construct a form of desire capable of jamming images of a better world into every fracture of daily life, from subway rides to service jobs to global poverty. In every moment of social suffering, this desire demands a better way of life. At the same time,

by making use of our broadest historical knowledge and deepest theoretical criticism, we have
to constantly ask ourselves how such desires
might lead to impasses that could be avoided.
Perhaps some kind of prophetic prosthesis is
required to transform the *desire for communism*
into a *communist desire*. Still, this desire only
deserves to be called "communist" if it can prove,
again and again, in every situation of domination and against every compromise, that even
more can be desired.[2]

future conflicts—conflicted future

So what is communism? Is it a society where
everybody receives the same wage, where
the bourgeois promise of equality is materi-
ally cashed out? Is it a society, as some critics
think, that reduces everything to the empty
equality of the lowest common denominator,
rewarding the lazy and hampering the hard-
working by removing "performance incen-
tives" (as we saw in trial no. 1)? Or rather, is
it a society where the means of production are
equally shared, including the property of those
who use them? Is it a society where everyone produces autonomously and trades fairly,

because money is abolished (trial no. 2)? Or is communism a society where class differences are leveled because it abolishes ownership of the means of production? Is it a society where each person receives just as much wealth as they have contributed to its production, that is, the full "proceeds of labor"—without reduction or exploitation? Is it thus a society where workers have everything—a workers' society (trial no. 3)? Or maybe communism names the society that has bid farewell to the superfluous, alienated consumer goods that dominate people's lives within capitalism—goods that nurture people's greed and distract them from what is essential. Maybe, then, it's a society that places people's true needs above the imperative to increase the productive forces (trial no. 5). Or then again, communism might be the society where politics recedes to the mere "administration of things." Maybe, because poverty has been abolished, and wealth bursts forth from every conceivable source, there is no longer any struggle over distribution. Is it a society that brings the struggle of labor to its historic end and realizes luxury for all, where champagne flows and molecular meals fly straight into idly opened mouths (trial no. 4)?[3] Is communism in fact a society where there is no longer any conflict—a time of harmony and stasis? Or is

communism the society in which prehistory has
ended and human history begins, where people
start to consciously make their *own* history? Is
communism, then, the beginning of politics—
the potential to decide our own fate, free from
the domination of dead labor, economic con-
straints, and autonomous structures (trial no.
6)? Is it a radically democratic society, then? Is
communism the cracking of the individual self,
the end of our isolation? Would communist
society subsume the particular under the universal? Or would it simply break with the compulsion to identify, and set free the nonidentical
by suspending the rule of blind averages? Would
we, the collective subject of humanity, through
communism, finally realize our own being by
appropriating a world that actually belongs to
us already, because we created it? Or is communism a community that can neither produce nor
present any work in common because it contains
no trace of a human essence to realize or rep-
resent?[4] Is it a community that has learned to
welcome rather than control the unavailability
of the social? Is communism, therefore, not an
appropriation but instead an "ex-appropriation"
without center and without unity—a *community
without unity*—where things, people, animals,
and others are connected in new ways?[5]

Meanwhile, the concept of communism has multiplied. Out of one communism, many communisms bloom. Rather than suggesting an actual communist pluralism, this tells us that the concept of communism is itself contested—that it names a field of political conflict. All these contradictory concepts of communism have been, or are presently, represented by libertarian or authoritarian communists, socialists, and anarchists. Undeniably, communism is always more than just the negation of capitalism. Right from the start, it's been intertwined with the critique of other communisms and other socialist utopias in a struggle over the future.

Despite all this, or maybe because of it, we can say that communism seeks to negate and not merely diminish the suffering unleashed by capitalist society. The various kinds of anticapitalist utopias can be reconstructed according to how much each proposed counterimage is still rooted in a capitalist model. When the critique underlying a particular image of utopia remains bound to the perspective of capitalism, then that utopia shows itself, unwillingly, to be a continuation of the status quo. This occurs when a critique idealizes a specific moment in capitalism and poses it against other moments in capitalism—thereby disarticulating its harmful character. Anticapitalist utopias can therefore be roughly distinguished on the basis of the following questions: What ideal do they trace out, and which sphere of the capitalist economy acts as the template for this ideal?

critique of critiques, negation of negations

circulation
The critique of capitalism whose criteria is the ideal of *simple commodity production* functions according to the classical form of immanent critique. It compares the ideals of the French Revolution—freedom and equality—with their inadequate realization. In this respect, it achieves a critique of bourgeois economy on the basis of bourgeois economy. As sociologist Nadja Rakowitz has shown, this underlying conception of freedom is liberal and bourgeois; it is the negative freedom of the individual—freedom from collective coercion and cooperation.[6] If freedom is defined positively, it's only considered as the freedom to consume or produce. This perspective assumes that everyone is free to decide on the products they consume and produce as individuals, alone, free from the influence of social conventions and plans. Moreover, the understanding of equality in this critique is based on the idea of equivalence or, economically

speaking, equilibrium. This is the equality of
indifferent commodity owners pitted against
each other whose supply and demand ideally
balances out.

As a critique leveled from the perspective of
the sphere of circulation, the core problem of
capitalism arises precisely at the point where
the reality of bourgeois society differs from its
ideals. This critique still clings to the concepts
of exchange and value, and presupposes production for sale: privately producing what others
consume, and privately consuming what others produce. Thus it grasps the buying and selling of the commodity called labor power as an
exchange of equivalents, a relation of equals. At
the end of the day, the "circulationist" critique
of capitalism can only denounce the origins
of surplus value as fraudulent—as a violation,
above all, of the law of equivalence. The perpe-
trator of this fraud is often identified as money,
or rather the financial market, whose own inter-
nal dynamic produces a growing gulf between
rich and poor.

On the economic level alone, this position
is already untenable. The problem of circula-
tionism lies in its attachment to the market.
Since the value of a product is only realized
after production, at the point of sale, there is
always a possibility for crisis. Under conditions

of market-based production, the presence and magnitude of society's demand for a particular commodity only become apparent in the market itself. The threat of collapse immediately appears for individual private producers when their economic calculus misfires, making them bankrupt. A whole repertoire of capitalist crises looms as a consequence, including the possibility of stagnation, overproduction, overaccumulation, and so on. Let us for now leave aside the problems of surplus value production and the reproduction of classes, which are not touched on here at all. Together with private production comes continuous competition. There is not only an incentive to produce as cheaply as possible but also a *compulsion* to do so, to outdo competitors, reduce wages, and in general, set in motion widening spirals of accumulation. In short, by eliminating or regulating money, the circulationists end up reproducing everything they set out to abolish.

We can more generously read the affirmation of the market that drives the circulationist critique as stemming from a strong distrust of forced collectivization or any planned attack by the collective against the individual. The sphere of circulation, in which people encounter each other as free and equal, is considered to be the guarantor of individual freedom. Such is the fetish character of commodity relations, which disarticulates the social character of production and reproduction, tempting us to perceive both as merely technical-economic prerequisites of exchange. Hidden from view in this fetishized perspective is how the market suspends personal, concrete forms of power only in order to replace them with an abstract form of power. Far from decreasing dependence between individuals, commodity production magnifies and globalizes it. Yet this interdependence remains reified. People do not understand or even perceive their relations with each other, and so they cannot shape them. It is not without some historical justification that liberal theorists of civil society cast suspicions of "totalitarianism" on the aim of comprehensively changing or democratically redesigning the social order of capitalism. Since they do not wish to characterize their ideals of equality and freedom as inherently bourgeois or capitalist, however, such theorists remain incapable of grasping the mediations of circulation in other spheres of the capitalist economy. In so doing, they reproduce all the relations of domination that uphold the sphere of circulation.

production
The most dominant strand of anticapitalist critique comes from the standpoint of the sphere

of production. While the representatives of circulationist theory mainly stem from left-liberal milieus and are thus often anticommunist, the fetishizing of production is traditionally a state-socialist phenomenon. In its classical version, the productivist critique of capitalism functions as a dualistic, unmediated confrontation between labor and capital. Abstracted from its specifically capital-determined form, "labor" is posited as something ahistorical and anthropological, with all kinds of ineluctable, progressive, and world-historical powers optimistically attributed to it. In contrast, capital is considered unproductive, as mere nonlabor, which does nothing other than unfairly appropriate the unpaid surplus labor of workers. The central category of this critique is therefore exploitation, understood distributively. The overcoming of capitalism occurs through juridical measures and state expropriation of the capitalist class, whereby the nonproductive elements of society are removed and all human beings become workers.

This perspective precludes the possibility of seeing labor itself as formally determined by capital; it also bars thinking of appropriation in anything other than legal or moral terms. The tension between forces and relations of production, treated here as identical to the labor/capital relation, is reduced to property relations. Hence, neither the specific nature of capitalist labor nor society's fixation on surplus production, on growth, is questioned. Social theorist Moishe Postone has shown how core capitalist categories survive relatively intact within such traditional party communism.[7] Labor, although an abstract concept, does not refer to an ahistorical practice. Rather, labor only becomes a generalized social reality with the emergence of the capitalist mode of production. Not until the rise of the factory, regulated workplace, and working day could the spheres of life and labor be separated. The construction of abstract time—time independent of the seasons, weather, traditional customs, and the particular needs of the object of labor—represents an indispensable condition for this division. The history of its enforcement is inextricably tied to the history of discipline. But the abstraction of labor relies on more than just the partition of work time from free time; it also depends on the separation of production from reproduction. The capitalist construction of labor is accompanied by the formation of two separate spheres, production and reproduction, which in turn necessitate two distinct social complexes of knowledge, activity and affect. And with that comes two distinct subjectivities, gendered and dichotomized.

The dehistoricization of labor means taking a historically specific form of labor, the *capitalist* form of labor, as ontological. In fact, only in capitalism is it even possible to speak of "labor" as such. Abstract labor is abstract both in the sense that it is cut off from other spheres and other moments of capitalism (for instance, reproduction), and insofar as it is subject to abstract time, being quantifiable and measurable to a precise degree. Abstract time assumes the logics of value and equivalence together with the attendant bourgeois concepts of equality and justice. Furthermore, labor emerges abstractly in history as a thing emptied of all its noninstrumental moments. Everything that does not serve the production of surplus value must be abstracted from it. Traditional Marxism seeks to vindicate "labor" as the positive antithesis to capital, turning a moment of capitalist society against itself. Yet this moment has been constructed by capital and obeys its laws.

consumption

Compared to productivist anticapitalism, the critique of capitalism from the standpoint of consumption is relatively new. Consumption first acquired significance for the Paris bohemians of the nineteenth century, later preoccupying the cultural critics of the 1920s, and finally only

becoming a mass phenomenon for the prole-
tariat with the development of Fordism. Indeed,
it was only in tandem with the crisis of Fordism in the 1960s and 1970s that the commodity form became the bearer of a revolutionary
promise of happiness—one that went beyond
the petty bourgeois ideal of an integrated working class pacified with homes, televisions, and
cars. When the postwar capitalist regime of
renewed accumulation went into crisis, so did
the Protestant, Prussian-style social frugality
that defined it. A cultural revolution spawned
in its wake, opening up fresh avenues of expansion for both capital and its critics. The lifting
of taboos surrounding sexuality and hedonism
generated new markets, marketing strategies,
and circuits of accumulation. An unprecedented
focus on reproduction opened up new territo-
ries for political struggle in the home, in the
party, and in the streets. At the same time, the
turn toward reproduction was undoubtedly the
historical effect of defeat within the factory. As
theorist Katja Diefenbach has shown, the "consumptionist" critique of capitalism exists at the
intersection of revolt and integration.[8]

The critique of capitalism from the standpoint of consumption argues that no criticism of
capitalism should lag behind its achievements.

That's why it opposes all puritan, ascetic, and ecological ideals. The social democratic slogan "the right to work" is transformed into "the right to be lazy."[9] Instead of full employment, it demands full unemployment, a universal basic income, and more free time.[10] Correspondingly, this view welcomes the progressive mechanization and full automation of production because it enlarges the possibilities of consumption, both through the expansion of production and reduction of labor time. The main line of consumptionist critique consists of accusing capitalism of being unable to fulfill the promise of happiness pledged to the masses.

While the slogan "luxury for all!" criticizes the exclusion of the majority of the world's population from social wealth, it nonetheless fails to bring into critical perspective the specific form of this wealth. Not only are questions of health and ecology left out; above all, this approach tacitly accepts the consumer monad, individualism of consumption, and separation of the spheres of consumption and production. By accepting this separation, this perspective mistakes emancipation for mechanization because it ignores the crucial question of the control, construction, and programming of machines.[11] Yet the sphere of consumption is every bit as much a product of modern capitalism as are the spheres of circulation and production. Objectively, its construction is necessary to locate demand for all produced commodities—that is, to keep accumulation going. Subjectively, its existence is necessary as compensation for alienated labor. While labor is construed as pure exertion, toil, or duty, the customer is as a queen whose freedom to choose is only limited quantitatively, by money. The qualitative limits of the consumer's options can only be expressed as three options: *buy*, *don't buy*, and *steal*. While labor is shaped by hierarchies of subordination to the pressures of the production process, the money commodity lends its possessor control over the labor time of others. That's why money bears a certain fetish of masculine autonomy. Capital shapes all products as commodities, whether in their particular durability, quality, and specificity, or symbolically in their branding, distinction, and standardization. The addiction to consumption as a sphere separated from production stands fundamentally at odds with full social emancipation. Criticizing capitalism from the standpoint of consumption extends the ideological function of accepting the promise of happiness by means of commodities. The goal is rather to collectively transform all social spheres so that the need to escape—into "leisure" time, the mall, or television—is overwhelmingly minimized.

printing a negative of the future

Thus ends the critique of critique(s). We've categorized the various criticisms of capitalism and associated (communist) utopias according to their various inadequacies. Each critique can be criticized from a communist standpoint simply because they each criticize capitalism from a latently capitalist standpoint—whether that of circulation, production, or consumption. Yet our own categorization and critique itself has a standpoint. Where does our standpoint stand, and who stands there? What kind of u-topos is this proposed communist vantage point, this place of no-place in capitalism? Is it a solid point to stand on, if one can stand on it at all? Or are these static terms wholly inadequate to the movement of communist critique, a form of criticism that runs forward, drifts backward, attacks sideways, and jumps away from any fixed position?

In *Minima Moralia*, critical theorist Theodor W. Adorno gives a paradoxical answer to the normative problem of the standpoint. He writes:

"The only philosophy which can be responsibly practiced in the face of despair is the attempt to contemplate all things as they would present themselves from the standpoint of redemption." It is "the utterly impossible thing, because it presupposes a standpoint removed, even though by a hair's breadth, from the scope of existence."[12] This perspective doesn't outright dismiss the figure of the standpoint but instead uproots it from the past, away from any origins, primitive communism, or matriarchy. Furthermore, this viewpoint refuses to be transhistorical, based in nature or anthropology. Rather, our only possible standpoint lies in the future. The hope is that the absurdity and unnecessary brutality of capitalist society will leap out to the people of future generations, the same way that the binary gender system or flatness of the earth seems crazy to us today. For Adorno, the demand to take up the standpoint of the future is emancipatory precisely because it's unattainable. The inviolability of the future keeps us from thinking that our thinking is unconstrained by the present. This idea of conceptual freedom prepares the ground on which the limits of bourgeois society can be expanded. "Thought must comprehend even its own impossibility for the sake of the possible."[13] The paradox that the external standpoint cannot be taken up and yet must be taken up protects us from fetishizing our own criticisms, and thus saves us from the illusion of utopianism: the fantasy that we can already show, here and now, what a liberated society looks like. In short, the unattainability of the communist viewpoint guards it from occupying capitalist ground. But how secure is this protection? Is the future as undisturbed by the present as Adorno proclaims? Doesn't the present constantly grasp at the future, just as the past constantly grasps at the present? Doesn't the concept of the future incessantly change as the actual future changes with every present transformation?

A transformation is a production of the future, a realization of a possibility as well as the creation and exclusion of possibilities. If the redemptive future negates the present suffering, then shouldn't the future and the idea of the future be constantly in flux? How could this negation remain the same if that which it negates is always changing? If communism cannot and must not remain undisturbed by history, then the prohibition on the representation of the future is nothing more than a fetish that encrypts communism as something undisturbed, indivisible, unsullied, and *supra*historical. Doesn't all this talk of the "future," of "liberation" and "redemption" obscure the point that none of these concepts could or should be identical to themselves—that

communism today means something quite different than what it did a hundred years ago, and
that tomorrow it will mean something different
yet again? "Communist critique cannot remain
indifferent to the transformation of power relations; it has a temporal core. What communism
means must be determined in every historical
situation anew."[14]

For Adorno, it is both impossible to take up
any future standpoint and simultaneously "the
simplest of all things, because the situation
calls imperatively for such knowledge, indeed
because consummate negativity, once squarely
faced, delineates the mirror-image of its oppo-
site."[15] But this delineation never comes. The
conceptual negation of negation does not auto-
matically become a position. The counterimage,
the negative sculpture of the future, cannot be
deduced from the critique of capitalism or critique of limited critiques of capitalism. Even the
sharpest photographic negative can make more
than one print. Hundreds of distinct images can
sometimes be generated, depending on exposure,
perspective, and technique. This critical over-
turning of the ban on representation acquires
surprising support from Adorno himself who,
in conversation with philosopher Ernst Bloch,
remarked, "Something terrible happens due to

the fact that we are forbidden to cast a picture. That is to say, firstly, concerning what ought to be: the more it can only be said negatively, the less definite one can imagine it. But then—and this is probably even more frightening—the commandment against a concrete expression of utopia tends to defame the utopian consciousness and to engulf it. What is really important, however, is the will *that* it is different."[16] At this point, Adorno encounters the thought of Michel Foucault, who in another conversation proclaimed, "In my opinion, the role of intellectuals today must be to restore the same level of desirability for the image of revolution that existed in the 19th century. To this end, necessarily new modes of human relations, that is, new modes of knowledge, new modes of desire and sexual life have to be invented."[17] It takes courage to speak out, to imagine, and to create an artificial object, a provisional utopia, an image of communism that can also inflame a communist desire. There's a lot at stake here. Since the less people are able to do what they want to do, the less they want to want anything at all. And how can people do what they want if they don't (want to) know what it is they want? When the scope of the possible limits what is desirable, then desire itself becomes desirable.

Desire must be invented, it must be wanted. *Desire desire*! Communist desire: the desire that misery finally comes to an end.

the beginning

It's not just the end of history that weighs like a nightmare on the desire for communism. Even more so, it's the end of revolution. Not just 1991, but also 1939 and 1937, and subsequently, 1924 and 1921, all the way to 1917. After all the failed attempts to realize a communist society in the twentieth century, can we still respond in good conscience with silence to the question of what communism should look like? Should we discuss communism without any reference to history? Can we so naively leap over the barrier between generations by seeking immediate, untainted access to Karl Marx's original manuscripts? Can those who coyly refuse to take responsibility for the legacy of Stalinism and its victims still be allowed to call themselves communists today? The cheap promise that "it will be more democratic next time" is just as empty as the claim that nothing can or should ever be said about what communism is to look like. Ideally, the ban on images of communism blocks the possibility of repeating the present in our dreams of the future, but in reality it's a lie that conceals the real possibility of falling into a traumatic repetition of the past. The dictum that the beautiful image of true communism can never be represented becomes, in short, the justification for closing one's eyes to the ugliness of real images of false communism.[18] It is as though it were up to an uncertain future and not communists themselves to provide an answer to the question, Why will the communism of the future not resemble the communism of the past?

This book was written during the end of history. Now, the end of history itself is history. Seen from the future, which has already started, this historic era will have begun in 1991 and have lasted exactly twenty years, until the Arab Spring in 2011. As with the great revolutionary cycles of the twentieth century—1917, 1968, and to a limited extent, 1989—the revolutions moved from city to city, from region to region, across national borders. And like those previous cycles, it all began at the periphery of the global order, pushing from there, more or less successfully, toward the center, to the "belly of the beast." From Sidi Bouzid to Cairo, and on to Benghazi, Daraa al-Manama, and Sana'a, across Athens, Madrid, Tel Aviv, London, Santiago de Chile, and Wisconsin, to New York, Frankfurt, Oakland, Moscow, Rio de Janeiro, and Istanbul, to Hong Kong and Rojava, on to Sarajevo and Paris. Many of the Russian revolutionaries of 1917 were convinced that they would succeed only if the revolution spread to the entire capitalist world. They set all their hopes on Germany—and were disappointed. Again today, Germany plays a special role, especially within Europe. With its politics of deflation, low wages, hard currency, and cheap exports, Germany has simultaneously contributed to the European crisis—which it now worsens by meting out austerity measures—and richly profited from it.

Today, once again, the success of revolutions depends on their ability to vitalize and radicalize one another along with their potential to globalize themselves. As undeniably different as the movements are from one another, their references to each other are obvious: digital mobilizing, the occupation of public squares—Tahrir Square, Plaza de Sol, Syntagma Square, Zuccotti Park, Taksim Square, Place de la République—a politics opposed to the state and, where possible, utilizing tactics of nonviolent protest. Above all, these revolts are characterized by a radical democratic form of organization that often excludes centralized institutions like parties while placing front and center a demand for social—that is to say, political and economic—democratization.

The global character of the revolutionary movements became visible when demonstrators in Egypt carried banners showing their solidarity with the striking workers in Wisconsin; when Taksim solidarity camps appeared in New York City as well as Athens and Berlin. One group now teaches another new forms of protest and organization. At the same time, this group may learn something from the fact that another group has adopted its strategies—for example, that the overthrow of a dictator or military council does not lead in itself to a democracy worthy of the name. To wit, just as Egyptian protesters had won freedom of the press, newspapers and public broadcasters in Greece were shut down because they were no longer profitable. We can also learn from previous cycles of struggles. In France, the occupation of the Place de la République—typical of the Occupy precursors and inspiration for the Nuit Debout movement—combined with political forms derived from the traditional vocabulary of French labor struggles: strikes at schools, oil refineries, and nuclear power plants, strikes by garbage collectors, and blockades in the transport sector. In Greece, a lesson from Argentina in 2001 was revived: the end to profitability does not have to mean the end of production. It can mean another beginning, too. The occupied factories, collective canteens, and self-governing hospitals can be understood as material attempts by people under the pressure of crisis to seek out the contours of another future together.[19] Isolated, they fail. So much depends on whether people manage to combine the numerous initiatives from below into new modes of relating with each other.

The current revolutionary movements, like many of their predecessors, are capable of their own forms of corruption, including anti-Semitism, misogyny, and nationalism. Concurrently, all over the world, fascist, reactionary, and Islamist movements are waiting for their opportunity to make history. From Poland, Croatia, and Hungary to Brazil, Turkey, Syria, and the United States, reactionary solutions to the crisis contain fresh policies of sexist segregation and racist exclusion. Furthermore, the strategies of military Keynesianism, suppression of competition, and "productive" destruction of capital—that is, war—have been and historically remain "successful." Rosa Luxemburg's famous dictum seems contemporary once again: socialism or barbarism. But historical socialism itself resulted in new forms of barbarism. In its world-historical attempt to abolish domination, socialism disgraced itself, painfully and poignantly. Today, however, with the world economic crisis at hand and emancipatory *or* reactionary movements brewing, the liberal-democratic model of capitalism has also lost much of the appeal it had twenty years ago. The "eternal present" of capital has ended, for now. Under conditions of crisis, there is no mere defense of the status quo. It is not enough to prevent the worst and get the bad. The most effective protection against the return of fascism is not to preserve the world it ostensibly fights, but to create a different world. The politics of separation can only be challenged by a politics of solidarity. For the first time in ages, history is open once again—for suggestions.

notes

1. Karl Marx and Friedrich Engels, *The German Ideology*, Marx Engels Collected Works 5 (New York: International Publishers, 1976), 49.

2. "Ein Wort zur Radikalität" ["A Word on Radicality"], *Sinistra! Radikale Linke*, 2003, www.copyriot.com/sinistra/reading/studi6 .html (accessed September 7, 2016).

3. Jürgen Dollase, "Dekonstruiert euch! Die Neuerungen, die Ferran Adrià in die Haute Cuisine eingebracht hat, sind heute überall sichtbar: Doch die wahre Revolution des Geschmacks steht noch bevor" ["Deconstruct Yourself! The Innovations That Ferran Adrià Introduced to Haute Cuisine Are Visible Everywhere Today: But the True Revolution of Taste Is Still to Come"] *Frankfurter Allgemeine*, January 3, 2009, 32.

4. Jean-Luc Nancy, *The Inoperative Community* (Minneapolis: University of Minnesota Press, 1991).

5. Jacques Derrida, "Politics and Friendship: An Interview with Michael Sprinker," in *The Althusserian Legacy*, edited by E. Ann Kaplan and Michael Sprinkler (London: Verso, 1993), 183–231; Donna J. Haraway, *Simians, Cyborgs, and Women: The Reinvention of Nature* (New York: Routledge, 1991).

6. Nadja Rakowitz, *Einfache Warenproduktion: Ideal und Ideologie* [*Simple Commodity-Production: Ideal and Ideology*] (Freiburg: ça-ira-Verlag, 2000).

7. Moishe Postone, *Time, Labor, and Social Domination: A Reinterpretation of Marx's Critical Theory* (Cambridge: Cambridge University Press, 1993).

8. Katja Diefenbach, "Alles ist gut: Warum eine Politik des Wunsches nichts damit zu tun hat, sich etwas zu wünschen" ["All Is Well: Why a Politics of Desire Has Nothing to Do with Desiring Anything"], *diskus*, March 2, 2003, 35–37.

9. This was the demand of Paul Lafargue, Marx's son-in-law.

10. Nick Srnicek and Alex Williams, *Inventing the Future: Postcapitalism and a World without Work* (London: Verso, 2015).

11. Biene Baumeister and Zwi Negator, *Situationistische Revolutionstheorie: Eine Aneignung, Vol. II: Kleines Organon* [*Situationist Theory of Revolution: An Appropriation, Vol. II: Small Organon*] (Stuttgart: Schmetterling Verlag, 2005), 97f.

12. Theodor W. Adorno, *Minima Moralia: Reflections from Damaged Life* (Frankfurt: Suhrkamp Verlag, 1970), §153.

13. Ibid.

14. *diskus*, "Simulate Communism," www.copyriot.com/diskus (accessed July 31, 2016).

15. Adorno, *Minima Moralia*, §153.

16. Ernst Bloch, "Something's Missing: A Discussion between Ernst Bloch and Theodor W. Adorno on the Contradictions of Utopian Longing (1964)," in Ernst Bloch, *The Utopian Function of Art and Literature* (Cambridge: MIT Press, 1988), 12, translation modified.

17. Michel Foucault, "Le savoir comme crime [Knowledge as crime]," interview with S. Terayama," in *Dits et écrits III* (Paris: Éditions Gallimard, 1994), 86.

18. Bini Adamczak, *Gestern Morgen: Über die Einsamkeit kommunistischer Gespenster und die Rekonstruktion der Zukunft* [*Past Future: On the Loneliness of Communist Specters and the Reconstruction of the Future*] (Münster: Unrast, 2007), 141.

19. Margarita Tsomou, "Last Exit. Zum Aufschwung solidarischer Ökonomien im Griechenland der Krise" ["Last Exit: On the Revival of Solidarity Economies in Crisis Greece"], *West-End: Neue Zeitschrift für Sozialforschung* 1 (2014), 79–92.